## DATE DUE

| | |
|---|---|
| OCT 0 7 2008 | |
| MAR 1 0 2009 | |
| APR 0 9 2009 | |
| | |
| | |
| | |
| | |
| | |
| | |
| | |
| | |
| | |
| | |
| | |
| | |

GAYLORD

PRINTED IN U.S.A.

# THE
# NIAGARA RIVER

# THE NIAGARA RIVER

*poems*

*by*
# KAY RYAN

GROVE PRESS • NEW YORK

*Published simultaneously in Canada*
*Printed in the United States of America*

Library of Congress Cataloging-in-Publication Data
Ryan, Kay.
      The Niagara River / Kay Ryan.
         p. cm.
      ISBN-10: 0-8021-4222-2
      ISBN-13: 978-0-8021-4222-1
      I. Title.
    PS3568.Y38N53 2005
    8.1'.54—dc21                          2005040423

Grove Press
an imprint of Grove/Atlantic, Inc.
841 Broadway
New York, NY 10003

08 09 10   10 9 8 7 6 5 4 3

*For Carol*

# CONTENTS

# ACKNOWLEDGMENTS

Grateful acknowledgment is made to the following publications in which these poems first appeared:

THE AMERICAN SCHOLAR: *Tired Blood; Still Life, with Her Things; Legerdemain; Nothing Getting Past*, THE ATLANTIC: *Hailstorm*, BOSTON REVIEW: *Caps*, MS.: *Late Justice; Hide and Seek*, THE NEW CRITERION: *The Well or the Cup; Thieves; The Material; Shipwreck*, THE NEW YORKER: *Green Hills; Things Shouldn't Be So Hard*, PARNASSUS: *The Self Is Not Portable*, POETRY: *Tenderness and Rot; Stardust; Post-Construction; Expectations; Home to Roost; The Niagara River; Backward Miracle; The Other Shoe; Least Action; Tune; Repulsive Theory; The Light of Interiors; Chinese Foot Chart; Sharks' Teeth; Carrying a Ladder; Almost Without Surface; Blue China Doorknob; Chop; The Best of It; Houdini; Duck; Latents; Rubbing Lamps; Felix Crow; Fake Spots; A Ball Rolls on a Point; He Lit a Fire with Icicles; Atlas; Thin; Tar Babies; Rats' Tails; On the Difficulty of Drawing Oneself Up; Salvage; Lighthouse Keeping*, SPEAKEASY: *Last Chance*, THREEPENNY REVIEW: *Absences and Breaks (originally titled Not News); No Names; The Past; The Elephant in the Room; Chart*, WATER/STONE: *Added Significance*, YALE REVIEW: *Desert Reservoirs; Theft; Weak Forces*, ZYZZYVA: *Ideal Audience*

"Home to Roost" also appeared in *The Best American Poetry 2005* (Scribners, 2005). "Chinese Foot Chart" was reprinted in *The Pushcart Prize XXIX* (Pushcart Press, 2005).

The author is deeply grateful to both the National Endowment for the Arts and the John Simon Guggenheim Memorial Foundation for the great help of their fellowships, and to The Poetry Foundation for the Ruth Lilly Poetry Prize.

# THE
# NIAGARA RIVER

# THE NIAGARA RIVER

As though
the river were
a floor, we position
our table and chairs
upon it, eat, and
have conversation.
As it moves along,
we notice—as
calmly as though
dining room paintings
were being replaced—
the changing scenes
along the shore. We
do know, we do
know this is the
Niagara River, but
it is hard to remember
what that means.

# HOME TO ROOST

The chickens
are circling and
blotting out the
day. The sun is
bright, but the
chickens are in
the way. Yes,
the sky is dark
with chickens,
dense with them.
They turn and
then they turn
again. These
are the chickens
you let loose
one at a time
and small—
various breeds.
Now they have
come home
to roost—all
the same kind
at the same speed.

# CARRYING A LADDER

We are always
really carrying
a ladder, but it's
invisible. We
only know
something's
the matter:
something precious
crashes; easy doors
prove impassable.
Or, in the body,
there's too much
swing or off-
center gravity.
And, in the mind,
a drunken capacity,
access to out-of-range
apples. As though
one had a way to climb
out of the damage
and apology.

# Sharks' Teeth

Everything contains some
silence. Noise gets
its zest from the
small shark's-tooth-
shaped fragments
of rest angled
in it. An hour
of city holds maybe
a minute of these
remnants of a time
when silence reigned,
compact and dangerous
as a shark. Sometimes
a bit of a tail
or fin can still
be sensed in parks.

## FELIX CROW

Crow school
is basic and
short as a rule—
just the rudiments
of *quid pro crow*
for most students.
Then each lives out
his unenlightened
span, adding his
bit of blight
to the collected
history of pushing out
the sweeter species;
briefly swaggering the
swagger of his
aggravating ancestors
down my street.
And every time
I like him
when we meet.

## WEAK FORCES

I enjoy an accumulating
faith in weak forces—
a weak faith, of course,
easily shaken, but also
easily regained—in what
starts to drift: all the
slow untrainings of the mind,
the sift left of resolve
sustained too long, the
strange internal shift
by which there's no knowing
if this is the road taken
or untaken. There are soft
affinities, possibly electrical;
lint-like congeries; moonlit
hints; asymmetrical pink
glowy spots that are not
the defeat of something,
I don't think.

# THE ELEPHANT IN THE ROOM

It isn't so much
a complete elephant
as an elephant
sense—perhaps
pillar legs supporting
a looming mass,
beyond which it's
mostly a guess.
In any case, we
manage with relative
ease. There are just
places in the room
that we bounce off
when we come up
against; not something
we feel we have to
announce.

# A Ball Rolls on a Point

The whole ball
of who we are
presses into
the green baize
at a single tiny
spot. An aural
track of crackle
betrays our passage
through the
fibrous jungle.
It's hot and
desperate. Insects
spring out of it.
The pressure is
intense, and the
sense that we've
lost proportion.
As though bringing
too much to bear
too locally were
our decision.

# THE BEST OF IT

However carved up
or pared down we get,
we keep on making
the best of it as though
it doesn't matter that
our acre's down to
a square foot. As
though our garden
could be one bean
and we'd rejoice if
it flourishes, as
though one bean
could nourish us.

## CHINESE FOOT CHART

Every part of us
alerts another part.
Press a spot in
the tender arch and
feel the scalp
twitch. We are no
match for ourselves
but our own release.
Each touch
uncatches some
remote lock. Look,
boats of mercy
embark from
our heart at the
oddest knock.

# SHIPWRECK

*I was shipwrecked beneath a stormless sky*
*in a sea shallow enough to stand up in.*
—*Fernando Pessoa*

They're laughable
when we get there—
the ultimate articulations
of despair: trapped
in a tub filling with
our own tears, strapped
to a breadstick mast
a mouse could chew
down, hopping around
the house in paper shackles
wrist and ankle. It's
always stagey. Being
lost is just one's fancy—
some cloth, some paste—
the essence of flimsy.
Therefore we
double don't know
why we don't take off
the Crusoe rags, step
off the island, bow
from the waist, accept
your kudos.

# THE OTHER SHOE

Oh if it were
only the other
shoe hanging
in space before
joining its mate.
If the undropped
didn't congregate
with the undropped.
But nothing can
stop the midair
collusion of the
unpaired above us
acquiring density
and weight. We
feel it accumulate.

# ATLAS

Extreme exertion
isolates a person
from help,
discovered Atlas.
Once a certain
shoulder-to-burden
ratio collapses,
there is so little
others can do:
they can't
lend a hand
with Brazil
and not stand
on Peru.

# He Lit a Fire with Icicles

*For W. G. Sebald, 1944–2001*

This was the work
of St. Sebolt, one
of his miracles:
he lit a fire with
icicles. He struck
them like a steel
to flint, did St.
Sebolt. It
makes sense
only at a certain
body heat. How
cold he had
to get to learn
that ice would
burn. How cold
he had to stay.
When he could
feel his feet
he had to
back away.

# Rats' Tails

*For Joseph Brodsky, 1940–1996*

*All that's left of him is rats' tails.*
*There's a fate I could envy.*
*—Joseph Brodsky*

Let's say
some day
all that's
left of him
is rats' tails,
just scattered
bits of script:
a loose *e*,
an *s* or two,
a *g*, an almost-
*n*. If he had
hands he'd
rub them as
the test begins:
to see how little
will suggest
the rat again.

## Added Significance

In the wake of
horrible events
each act or word
is fortified with
added significance,
unabsorbable as
nutrients added
to the outside
of food: it can't
do any good.
As if significance
weren't burdensome
enough. Now
the wave-slapped
beach rocks not
just made to talk
but made to *teach*.

# Chop

The bird
walks down
the beach along
the glazed edge
the last wave
reached. His
each step makes
a perfect stamp—
smallish, but as
sharp as an
emperor's chop.
Stride, stride,
goes the emperor
down his wide
mirrored promenade
the sea bows
to repolish.

## Desert Reservoirs

They are beachless
basins, steep-edged
catches, unnatural
bodies of water wedged
into canyons, stranded
anti-mirages
unable to vanish
or moisten a landscape
of cactus adapted
to thrift, a wasteland
to creatures who chew
one another or grasses
for moisture. Nothing
here matches their gift.

# HAILSTORM

Like a storm
of hornets, the
little white planets
layer and relayer
as they whip around
in their high orbits,
getting more and
more dense before
they crash against
our crust. A maelstrom
of ferocious little
fists and punches,
so hard to believe
once it's past.

# EXPECTATIONS

We expect rain
to animate this
creek: these rocks
to harbor gurgles,
these pebbles to
creep downstream
a little, those leaves
to circle in the
eddy, the stains
and gloss of wet.
The bed is ready
but no rain yet.

# GREEN HILLS

Their green flanks
and swells are not
flesh in any sense
matching ours,
we tell ourselves.
Nor their green
breast nor their
green shoulder nor
the languor of their
rolling over.

# Rubbing Lamps

Things besides
Aladdin's and
the golden cave
fish's lamps
grant wishes.
In fact,
most lamps
aren't lamp-
shaped and
happen by
accident: an
ordinary knob
goes lambent
as you twist
or a cloth turns
to silver mesh
against a dish—
something
so odd and

filled with promise
for a minute
that you spend
your only wish
wishing someone else
could see it.

# TENDERNESS AND ROT

Tenderness and rot
share a border.
And rot is an
aggressive neighbor
whose iridescence
keeps creeping over.

No lessons
can be drawn
from this however.

One is not
two countries.
One is not meat
corrupting.

It is important
to stay sweet
and loving.

# TAR BABIES

Tar babies are
not the children
of tar people.
It is far worse.
The tar baby occurs
spontaneously
nor do we adhere
at first. There is
an especially
unperverse
attractiveness
to the tar baby—
although currently
she is a little sick.
When you start
to help her
is when she
starts to stick.

# TIRED BLOOD

Well, not *tired*
so much as *freighted*.
As though foreign objects
had invaded.
As though tiny offices
had dumped
their metal furniture
among the glossy lozenges
and platelets—
chairs that stick together,
painful cabinets.

# THEFT

The egg-sucking fox
licks his copper chops.
The shell cups
lie scattered from
the orange debauch.

It is honest
straightforward theft—
unlike whatever
cruel thing
steals *thought*

the full weight left
and the locked room
still locked.

# IDEAL AUDIENCE

Not scattered legions,
not a dozen from
a single region
for whom accent
matters, not a seven-
member coven,
not five shirttail
cousins; just
one free citizen—
maybe not alive
now even—who
will know with
exquisite gloom
that only we two
ever found this room.

# Caps

People should be
open on top like a cup.
A piece of bread
should be able to sop
some of us up.
We should be milk-like
or like wine. We should
not have to be trying
to get our caps off all the time.
The storybook boy
attempts the simple gesture
of baring his head
for his emperor,
but another hat has appeared.
This happens over and over.
Who does not share
his despair of simplicity,
of acting clearly and with dignity?
And what pleasure can we find
in the caps, brightly feathered
and infinitely various,
that pile up so high they bury us?

# THIN

How anything
is known
is so thin—
a skin of ice
over a pond
only birds might
confidently walk
upon. A bird's
worth of weight
or one bird-weight
of Wordsworth.

# STARDUST

Stardust is
the hardest thing
to hold out for.
You must
make of yourself
a perfect plane—
something still
upon which
something settles—
something like
sugar grains on
something like
metal, but with
none of the chill.
It's hard to explain.

# REPULSIVE THEORY

Little has been made
of the soft skirting action
of magnets reversed,
while much has been
made of attraction.
But is it not this pillowy
principle of repulsion
that produces the
doily edges of oceans
or the arabesques of thought?
And do these cutout coasts
and in-curved rhetorical beaches
not baffle the onslaught
of the sea or objectionable people
and give private life
what small protection it's got?
Praise then the oiled motions
of avoidance, the pearly
convolutions of all that
slides off or takes a
wide berth; praise every
eddying vacancy of Earth,

all the dimpled depths
of pooling space, the whole
swirl set up by fending off—
extending far beyond the personal,
I'm convinced—
immense and good
in a cosmological sense:
unpressing us against
each other, lending
the necessary *never*
to never-ending.

# Blue China Doorknob

*I was haunted by the image of a blue china doorknob.*
*I never used the doorknob, or knew what it meant,*
*yet somehow it started the current of images.*
—Robert Lowell

Rooms may be
using us. We
may be the agents
of doorknobs'
purposes, obeying
imperatives china
dreams up or
pacing dimensions
determined by
cabinets. And if
we're their instruments—
the valves of their
furious trumpets,
conscripted but
ignorant of it—
the strange, unaccountable
things we betray
were never our secrets
anyway.

# SALVAGE

The wreck
is a fact.
The worst
has happened.
The salvage trucks
back in and
the salvage men
begin to sort
and stack,
whistling as
they work.
Thanks be
to God—again—
for extractable elements
which are not
carriers of pain,
for this periodic
table at which
the self-taught
salvagers disassemble
the unthinkable
to the unthought.

# ALMOST WITHOUT SURFACE

Sometimes before
going to sleep a person
senses the give
behind the last given,

almost physically,
like the strain
of plush against
a skin.

The person imagines
a fig or peach,
perhaps a woman or
a deep constellation:
some fathomless
fruit.

But we are each
that, while we live,
however much
we resist: almost

without surface, barely
contained,

but crazy
as clouds compounding
each other, refusing
to rain.

# THE LIGHT OF INTERIORS

The light of interiors
is the admixture
of who knows how many
doors ajar, windows
casually curtained,
unblinded or opened,
oculi set into ceilings,
wells, ports, shafts,
loose fits, leaks,
and other breaches
of surface. But, in
any case, the light,
once in, bounces
toward the interior,
glancing off glassy
enamels and polishes,
softened by the scuffed
and often-handled, muffled
in carpet and toweling,
buffeted down hallways,
baffled equally

by the scatter and order
of love and failure
to an ideal and now
sourceless texture which,
when mixed with silence,
makes of a simple
table with flowers
an island.

# Things Shouldn't Be So Hard

A life should leave
deep tracks:
ruts where she
went out and back
to get the mail
or move the hose
around the yard;
where she used to
stand before the sink,
a worn-out place;
beneath her hand
the china knobs
rubbed down to
white pastilles;
the switch she
used to feel for
in the dark
almost erased.
Her things should
keep her marks.
The passage

of a life should show;
it should abrade.
And when life stops,
a certain space—
however small—
should be left scarred
by the grand and
damaging parade.
Things shouldn't
be so hard.

# The Past

Sometimes there's
suddenly no way
to get from
one part to
another, as though
the past were
a frozen lake
breaking up. But
not from the
top; not because
it's warmer
up here; it's not.
But from underneath
for some reason—
perhaps some heat
trapped on its own
for so long it's
developed seasons.

# Reverse Drama

Lightning, but not bright.
Thunder, but not loud.
Sometimes something
in the sky connects
to something in the ground
in ways we don't expect
and more or less miss except
through reverse drama:
things were heightened
and now they're calmer.

# FAKE SPOTS

Like air
in rocks, fake
spots got here
really far back.
Everything is
part caulk.
Some apartments
in apartment blocks
are blanks;
some steeples
are shims. Also
in people: parts
are wedges: and,
to the parts they keep
apart, *precious.*

# LEGERDEMAIN

Some days one gets
the *in* but not
the *out* part of the
rabbit/hat trick.
And the longer
a creature stays,
the worse it sticks.
Dispatch means
so much, one
remembers again.
A thing can get
too conjured
for legerdemain.

# HOUDINI

Each escape
involved some art,
some hokum, and
at least a brief
incomprehensible
exchange between
man and metal
during which the
chains were not
so much broken
as he and they
blended. At the
end of each such
mix he had to
extract himself. It
was the hardest
part to get right
routinely: breaking
back into the
same Houdini.

# Hide and Seek

It's hard not
to jump out
instead of
waiting to be
found. It's
hard to be
alone so long
and then hear
someone come
around. It's
like some form
of skin's developed
in the air
that, rather
than have torn,
you tear.

# LEAST ACTION

Is it vision
or the lack
that brings me
back to the principle
of least action,
by which in one
branch of rabbinical
thought the world
might become the
Kingdom of Peace not
through the tumult
and destruction necessary
for a New Start but
by adjusting little parts
a little bit—turning
a cup a quarter inch
or scooting up a bench.
It imagines an
incremental resurrection,
a radiant body
puzzled out through

tinkering with the fit
of what's available.
As though what is is
right already but
askew. It is tempting
for any person who would
like to love what she
can do.

# PITCHER

A pitcher molds
the air in it, dividing
from the air beyond
the air it holds. And
should the pitcher
vanish, something
would take a minute
to escape, a gradually
diminishing integrity,
a thinning pitcherful
of pitcher shape.

# POST-CONSTRUCTION

Who knows better
than the builder
not to trust
a structure, where
it's off kilter,
how too few
rafters bear
too much roof?

And still it
may stand, proof
against craft,
strong as though
ghost ribs
had been added
after one left.

# CHART

There is a big
figure, your age,
crawling, then
standing, now
beginning to bend
as he crosses
the stage. Or
she. A blurred
and generalized
projection of you
and me. For a
long time it seems
as remote
from the self
as the ape chart
where they rise up
and walk into man.
And then it seems
the realer part.

# NOTHING GETTING PAST

If life is a
thin film
sandwiched
between twin
immensities
of nothing,
you get the best
taste of this
out west in
the open country
where a keen
could mean the
double scrape
of nothing almost
touching nothing
or the wind
coming through
dry grass. In
either case it's
pretty close
to nothing
getting past.

# THE MATERIAL

*The ratio between the material Cornell collected
and the material that ended up in his boxes
was probably a thousand to one.*
—*Deborah Solomon,* Utopia Parkway

Whatever is done
leaves a hole in the
possible, a snip in
the gauze, a marble
and thimble missing
from the immaterial.
The laws are cruel
on this point. The
undone can't be
patched or stretched.
The wounds last.
The bundles of
nothing that are
our gift at birth, the
lavish trains we
trail into our span
like vans of seamless
promise, like fresh
sheets in baskets,
are our stock. We
must extract parts

to do work. As
time passes, the
promise is tattered
like a battle flag
above a war we
hope mattered.

# The Self Is Not Portable

The self is not
portable. It
cannot be packed.
It comes sneaking
back to any place
from which it's
been extracted,
for it is nothing alone.
It is not an entity.
The ratio of self
to home: one part
in seventy.

# ON THE DIFFICULTY OF
# DRAWING ONESELF UP

One does not stack.
It would be like
a mouse on the back
of a mouse
on a mouse's back.
Courses of mice,
layers of shivers
and whiskers,
a wobbling tower
mouse-wide,
with nothing more
than a mouse inside.

# DUCK

It isn't ever
all green thought
in green shade,
is it? When even
a duck pivots
beak-down in
pursuit of the
succulent options
that tuck and
cling among the
dangling roots of
an emerald dream,
parts stay so
independent they seem
foreign. With the
duck, for example,
the improbable
curl-peaked
eider island
that bobbles
above him.

# LAST CHANCE

*No more water*
*for 80 miles*
*or gas or*
*beer. If you*
*need some*
*get it here.*

It's just a gap
between stations,
a serviceless
hiatus—only
your last chance
in that sense—
really no more than
a glimpse.

# No Names

There are high places
that don't invite us,
sharp shapes, glacier-
scraped faces, whole
ranges whose given names
slip off. Any such relation
as we try to make
refuses to take. Some
high lakes are not for us,
some slick escarpments.
I'm giddy with thinking
where thinking can't stick.

# STILL LIFE, WITH HER THINGS

Today her things are quiet
and do not reproach,
each in its place,
washed in the light
that encouraged the Dutch
to paint objects as though
they were grace—
the bowl, the
goblet, the vase
from Delft—each
the reliquary
of itself.

# THE WELL OR THE CUP

How can
you tell
at the start
what you
can give away
and what
you must hold
to your heart.
What is
the well
and what is
a cup. Some
people get
drunk up.

# Charms

The dead do not
become stars or ghosts.
In fact, they are
hardly undone.
Soon their randomly
dispersed parts
reappear one
by one on
foreign hosts—
the beloved ear
or freckled arm,
separate as a
*milagro* or bracelet
charm. It is not
grotesque, though
odd. Even a piece
does us some good.

# ABSENCES AND BREAKS

It's what we can't
know that interests
us—the pre-Greeks
or Australopithecus—
where there are more
absences and breaks
than bits of bone
or pot. It's not
news, but it
fascinates—our
love of hints, our
mending minds that
love to patch up
other times like
plates, and how this
might extrapolate
to hearts: explaining
how here can be
too much matching part.

# LIGHTHOUSE KEEPING

Seas pleat
winds keen
fogs deepen
ships lean no
doubt, and
the lighthouse
keeper keeps
a light for
those left out.
It is intimate
and remote both
for the keeper
and those afloat.

# LATENTS

Just the hints, say
the side ridges of
fingerprints that
don't rule out
innocence; or
the loose approaches
to tightening mazes;
ambiguous, smudgy
places. The dilation
dark absorbs; the
thing we don't
think through
before it happens:
all the early
stations of desire—
the first slight tug
against the string
that threads the
wire that threads
the cable that
guys the bridge
that alien traffic
plies.

# TUNE

Imagine a sea
of ultramarine
suspending a
million jellyfish
as soft as moons.
Imagine the
interlocking uninsistent
tunes of drifting things.
This is the deep machine
that powers the lamps
of dreams and accounts
for their bluish tint.
How can something
so grand and serene
vanish again and again
without a hint?

# Late Justice

Late justice may
be more useless
than none. Some
expungings or
making-rights
or getting-backs
lack the capacity
to correct. The
formerly aggrieved
become exacting
in unattractive
ways: intolerant
of delay, determined
to collect. And shocked—
shocked—at their
new unappeasableness,
who had so long
been so reasonable.

# Backward Miracle

Every once in a while
we need a
backward miracle
that will strip language,
make it *hold* for
a minute: just the
vessel with the
wine in it—
a sacramental
refusal to multiply,
reclaiming the
single loaf
and the single
fish thereby.

# THIEVES

There are thieves
in the mind, their
dens in places
we'd prefer
not to know.
When a word
is lifted from
its spot, we show
no surprise,
replacing *supplies*
with *provender.*
Out here, it's
the tiniest stutter,
the subtlest patch—
an affordable loss
of no significance
whatever to the
plastic surface of
social commerce.
Should a bit vanish
from an event, we

likewise manage.
But back at the ranch,
a hoard is building.
The thieves are
hatching some
fantastic plot
made out of parts
we'd laugh to think
that they thought
matched.

# Green Behind the Ears

I was still slightly
fuzzy in shady spots
and the tenderest lime.
It was lovely, as I
look back, but not
at the time. For it is
hard to be green and
take your turn as flesh.
So much freshness
to unlearn.